Are We There Yet?
ALL About the Planet Mercury!
Space for Kids

Children's Aeronautics & Space Book

BABY PROFESSOR

EDUCATION KIDS

Speedy Publishing LLC

40 E. Main St. #1156

Newark, DE 19711

www.speedypublishing.com

Copyright 2016

FACTS ABOUT PLANET MERCURY

Mercury was named
after the Roman
God of Commerce
and Travel.

Mercury is the closest planet to the sun.

Mercury is the smallest planet in the solar system.

Planet Earth has 365 days in a year while mercury only has 88 days.

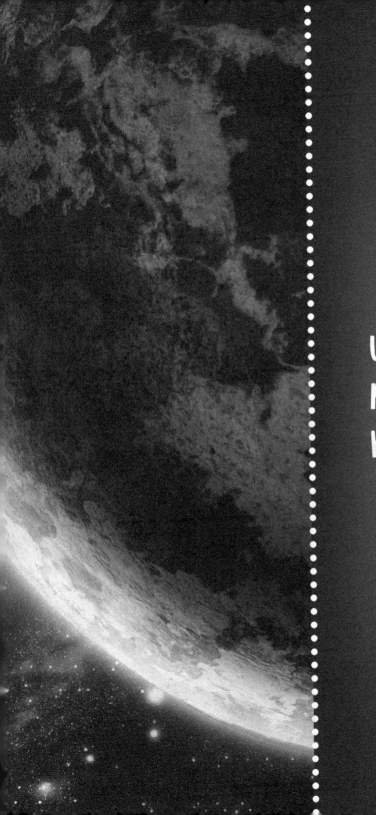

Unlike Earth,
Mercury does not
have a moon

Unlike Saturn, Mercury does not have rings.

SUN

MERCURY

VENUS

EARTH

MARS

JUPITER

SATURN

URANUS

NEPTUNE

Mercury and our
moon has a simiLar
surface.

Though Mercury's surface is rough. It still has regions with smooth plains.

Mercury is the second densest planet next to Earth.

Mercury is the second hottest planet next to Venus.

Mercury does
not have weather
and air because
it does not have
atmosphere.

The surface of
Mercury is full of
wrinkles.

There is no water
in the surface of
Mercury.

Since Mercury
is very near to
the sun, the
temperature is
extremely hot
during daytime.

During night time, the temperature of Mercury drops due to the absence of an atmosphere.

Just Like Earth, Mercury has light elements like sulfur.

Of the 8 planets in the Solar System, Mercury has the most craters.

Mariner 10 is the first spacecraft to map Mercury.

Visit

BABY PROFESSOR
EDUCATION KIDS

www.BabyProfessorBooks.com

to download Free Baby Professor eBooks
and view our catalog of new and exciting
Children's Books

CPSIA information can be obtained
at www.ICGtesting.com
Printed in the USA
BVHW060926230922
647619BV00004B/228